• *Cooking for Today* •

SOUPS & BROTHS

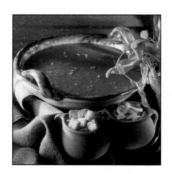

· Cooking for Today ·

SOUPS & BROTHS

ROSEMARY WADEY

· PARRAGON ·

First published in Great Britain in 1996 by
Parragon Book Service Ltd
Unit 13–17
Avonbridge Trading Estate
Atlantic Road
Avonmouth
Bristol BS11 9QD

ISBN 0-7525-1800-3

Produced by Haldane Mason

Printed in Italy

Acknowledgements:
Art Direction: Ron Samuels
Editor: Vicky Hanson
Series Design: Pedro & Frances Prá-Lopez/Kingfisher Design, London
Page Design: Somewhere Creative
Photography: Joff Lee
Styling: Maria Kelly
Home Economist: Rosemary Wadey

Photographs on pages 6, 18, 34, 48 and 60 reproduced by permission of
ZEFA Picture Library (UK) Ltd.

Note:
Cup measurements in this book are for American cups. Tablespoons are assumed to be 15 ml.
Unless otherwise stated, milk is assumed to be full-fat, eggs are standard size 2 and
pepper is freshly ground black pepper.

Contents

CHAPTER ONE

Chilled Soups

Of all the hundreds of types of soup, chilled soups must be the most elegant. They are most likely to be served in the summer, or at least on a warm day, and probably for some kind of entertaining, rather than just an everyday meal. Chilled soups have delicate flavours, often enhanced by a particular herb, and are usually smooth and velvety, although a little texture is often added by stirring in some chopped or grated ingredients, such as in Gazpacho (see page 8).

Vegetables, fish, seafood, meats, poultry and fruit all feature in chilled soups, so they can be made to suit any kind of meal and for all tastes. Chilled soups are often finished with cream, fromage frais or yogurt, either stirred into the soup before serving or swirled or spooned on top as an attractive garnish.

On a really hot day, a little finely crushed ice can be added just before serving the soup, but don't overdo it or it will dilute the soup too much. Most recipes can double up as delicious hot soups to serve throughout the year. Good accompaniments to chilled soups are all types of warmed bread or rolls, Garlic or Herb Bread (see page 76), Scones (see page 77) or Melba Toast (see page 32).

Opposite: A chilled soup is the perfect first course for a lunch 'al fresco'.

GAZPACHO

*This favourite Spanish soup is full of chopped and grated vegetables
with a puréed tomato base and is served with extra chopped vegetables
and Garlic Croûtons (see page 79).*

STEP 1

STEP 2

STEP 3

STEP 5

SERVES 4

¹/₂ small cucumber
¹/₂ small green (bell) pepper, chopped very
*   finely*
500 g/1 lb ripe tomatoes, skinned or
*   425 g/14 oz can chopped tomatoes*
¹/₂ onion, chopped coarsely
2–3 garlic cloves, crushed
3 tbsp olive oil
2 tbsp white wine vinegar
1–2 tbsp lemon or lime juice
2 tbsp tomato purée (paste)
450 ml/³/₄ pint/scant 2 cups tomato juice
salt and pepper

TO SERVE:
chopped green (bell) pepper
thinly sliced onion rings
Garlic Croûtons (see page 79)

1 Coarsely grate the cucumber into a
bowl and add the chopped green
(bell) pepper.

2 Blend the tomatoes, onion and
garlic in a food processor or
blender, then add the oil, vinegar, lemon
or lime juice and tomato purée (paste)
and blend until smooth. Alternatively,
finely chop the tomatoes and finely grate
the onion, then mix both with the garlic,
oil, vinegar, lemon or lime juice and
tomato purée (paste).

3 Add the tomato mixture to the
cucumber and green (bell) pepper
and mix well, then add the tomato juice
and mix again.

4 Season to taste, cover the bowl
with clingfilm (plastic wrap) and
chill thoroughly – for at least 6 hours
and preferably longer for the flavours to
meld together.

5 Prepare the side dishes and arrange
in individual bowls.

6 Ladle the soup into bowls,
preferably from a soup tureen set
on the table with the side dishes around
it. Hand the dishes around to allow the
guests to help themselves.

SERVING SUGGESTION

Hot Garlic or Herb Bread (see page 76)
makes a good accompaniment.

8

VICHYSSOISE

This is a classic creamy soup made from potatoes and leeks. To achieve the delicate pale colour, be sure to use only the white parts of the leeks. Vichyssoise is also excellent served hot.

STEP 1

STEP 2

STEP 3

STEP 5

SERVES 4–6

3 large leeks
45 g/ 1½ oz/ 3 tbsp butter or margarine
1 onion, sliced thinly
500 g/ 1 lb potatoes, chopped
900 ml/ 1½ pints/ 3½ cups Chicken or
  Vegetable Stock (see pages 77–78)
2 tsp lemon juice
pinch of ground nutmeg
¼ tsp ground coriander
1 dried bay leaf
1 egg yolk
150 ml/ ¼ pint/ ⅔ cup single (light) cream
salt and white pepper
snipped chives or crisply fried and crumbled
  bacon to garnish

1 Trim the leeks and remove most of the green part (it can be served as a vegetable). Slice the white part of the leeks very finely.

2 Melt the butter or margarine in a saucepan and fry the leeks and onion gently for about 5 minutes without browning, stirring from time to time.

3 Add the potatoes, stock, lemon juice, seasoning, nutmeg, coriander and bay leaf to the pan and bring to the boil. Cover and simmer for

about 30 minutes until all the vegetables are very soft.

4 Cool the soup a little, discard the bay leaf and then press through a sieve (strainer) or blend in a food processor or blender until smooth. Pour into a clean pan.

5 Blend the egg yolk into the cream, add a little of the soup to the mixture and then whisk it all back into the soup and reheat gently without boiling. Adjust seasoning to taste. Cool and chill thoroughly.

6 Serve the soup sprinkled with snipped chives or crisply fried and crumbled bacon.

VARIATION

To serve the soup hot, add the thinly sliced green part of the leeks after sieving (straining) or puréeing, then simmer for another 5–10 minutes until tender. Add just the cream (omit the egg yolk) and reheat gently.

STEP 2

STEP 3

STEP 4

STEP 5

AVOCADO & MINT SOUP

A rich and creamy pale green soup made with avocados and enhanced by a touch of chopped mint. Serve chilled in summer or hot in winter.

SERVES 4–6

45 g/1½ oz/3 tbsp butter or margarine
6 spring onions (scallions), sliced
1 garlic clove, crushed
30 g/1 oz/¼ cup plain (all-purpose) flour
600 ml/1 pint/2½ cups Chicken Stock (see page 77)
2 ripe avocados
2–3 tsp lemon juice
good pinch of grated lemon rind
150 ml/¼ pint/⅔ cup milk
150 ml/¼ pint/⅔ cup single (light) cream
1–1½ tbsp chopped fresh mint
salt and pepper
sprigs of fresh mint to garnish

MINTED GARLIC BREAD:
125 g/4 oz/½ cup butter
1–2 tbsp chopped fresh mint
1–2 garlic cloves, crushed
1 wholemeal (wholewheat) or white French loaf

1 Melt the butter or margarine in a large saucepan, add the spring onions (scallions) and garlic and fry gently for about 3 minutes until soft but not coloured.

2 Stir in the flour and cook for a minute or so. Gradually stir in the stock then bring to the boil. Leave to simmer gently while preparing the avocados.

3 Peel the avocados, discard the stones (pits) and chop coarsely. Add to the soup with the lemon juice and rind and seasoning. Cover and simmer for about 10 minutes until tender.

4 Cool the soup slightly then press through a sieve (strainer) or blend in a food processor or blender until smooth. Pour into a bowl.

5 Stir in the milk and cream, adjust the seasoning, then stir in the mint. Cover and chill thoroughly.

6 To make the minted garlic bread, soften the butter and beat in the mint and garlic. Cut the loaf into slanting slices but leave a hinge on the bottom crust. Spread each slice with the butter and reassemble the loaf. Wrap in foil and place in a preheated oven at 180°C/350°F/Gas Mark 4 for about 15 minutes.

7 Serve the soup garnished with a sprig of mint and accompanied by the minted garlic bread.

SPICED APPLE & APRICOT SOUP

This delicately flavoured fruit soup is gently spiced with ginger and allspice, and finished with a swirl of soured cream. Serve well chilled on a warm summer's day.

STEP 1

SERVES 4–6

125 g/4 oz/²/₃ cup dried apricots, soaked overnight or no-need-to-soak dried apricots
500 g/1 lb dessert apples, peeled, cored and chopped
1 small onion, chopped
1 tbsp lemon or lime juice
700 ml/1¼ pints/3 cups Chicken Stock (see page 77)
150 ml/¼ pint/²/₃ cup dry white wine
¼ tsp ground ginger
good pinch of ground allspice
salt and pepper

TO GARNISH:
4–6 tbsp soured cream or natural fromage frais
little ground ginger or ground allspice

1 Drain the apricots, if necessary, and chop.

2 Put in a saucepan and add the apples, onion, lemon or lime juice and stock.

3 Bring to the boil, cover and simmer gently for about 20 minutes until all the fruit is soft and broken down.

4 Leave the soup to cool a little, then press through a sieve (strainer) or blend in a food processor or blender until smooth. Pour the soup into a clean pan.

5 Add the wine and spices and season to taste. Bring back to the boil, then leave to cool. If too thick, add a little more stock or water and then chill thoroughly.

6 Put a spoonful of soured cream or fromage frais on top of each portion and lightly dust with ginger or allspice.

STEP 2

STEP 4

FRUIT SOUPS

Other fruits can be combined with apples to make fruit soups — try raspberries, blackberries, blackcurrants or cherries. If the fruits have a lot of pips or stones (pits), the soup should be sieved (strained) after puréeing.

STEP 5

STEP 1

STEP 2

STEP 3

STEP 5

CURRIED PRAWN (SHRIMP) SOUP

This soup is only lightly spiced with curry so the flavour of the prawns (shrimp) is not overpowered. The extra flavouring of almonds and coconut adds an exotic touch.

SERVES 4

2 tbsp ground almonds
2 tbsp unsweetened desiccated (shredded) coconut
150 ml/¼ pint/⅔ cup boiling water
60 g/2 oz/¼ cup butter or margarine
1 onion, minced or chopped very finely
2 celery sticks, minced (ground) or chopped very finely
30 g/1 oz /¼ cup plain (all-purpose) flour
1½ tsp medium curry powder
600 ml/1 pint/2½ cups Fish or Vegetable Stock (see pages 77–8)
2 tsp lemon or lime juice
3–4 drops Tabasco sauce
1 dried bay leaf
90–125 g/3–4 oz/½–⅓ cup peeled prawns (shrimp), thawed if frozen
300 ml/½ pint/1¼ cups milk
4–6 tbsp double (heavy) cream
salt and pepper

TO GARNISH:
4 whole prawns (shrimp)
chopped fresh parsley

1 Put the almonds and coconut into a bowl. Pour on the water, mix well and leave until cold. Strain, pushing down firmly with a potato masher or the back of a spoon, and reserve the liquor.

2 Melt the butter or margarine in a large saucepan. Add the onion and celery and fry gently for 3–4 minutes until soft but not coloured.

3 Stir in the flour and curry powder and cook gently for 2 minutes, then add the stock and coconut liquor and bring to the boil.

4 Add the lemon or lime juice, Tabasco, seasoning and bay leaf, cover and simmer for 10 minutes. Coarsely chop half the prawns (shrimp), add to the soup and simmer for a further 10 minutes.

5 Discard the bay leaf, stir in the milk and remaining prawns (shrimp) and bring back to the boil. Simmer for 3–4 minutes. Adjust the seasoning and stir in the cream. Chill thoroughly.

6 Garnish with prawns (shrimp) and chopped parsley and serve.

FREEZING

Do not freeze this soup if the prawns (shrimp) have been previously frozen.

CHAPTER TWO

Vegetable Soups

There is a huge variety of vegetable-based soups, so this chapter only covers a small selection. Vegetable soups can be rich and creamy or light and delicate. The vegetables are often puréed to give a smooth consistency and thicken the soup, but you can also purée just half the mixture, to give it more texture. Clear soups, such as French Onion Soup (see page 20) and Bortsch (see page 22) are often based on a richly flavoured stock. For vegetarians these soups should be made with a vegetable stock, but meat-eaters can use a good home-made chicken or meat stock, if preferred.

Try these recipes first then you can adapt them to make use of other vegetables – choose ingredients that are in season and soup-making can be extremely economical.

Opposite: Cooking vegetables in a soup ensures little of their goodness is lost.

FRENCH ONION SOUP

This classic French soup is packed with onions, which are cooked very slowly until they caramelize, which gives the soup its authentic rich flavour. It is traditionally served with toasted cheese croûtes.

STEP 1

STEP 2

STEP 3

STEP 5

SERVES 4

30 g/1 oz/2 tbsp butter or margarine
2 tbsp oil
500 g/1 lb onions, sliced thinly
1–2 garlic cloves, crushed
1 litre/1¾ pints/4 cups strong Beef or
    Vegetable Stock (see pages 76–8)
2 bay leaves, preferably fresh
1 tbsp brown sugar
1 tbsp white wine vinegar
good pinch of ground allspice
8 thin slices French bread
60 g/2 oz/½ cup Gruyere, Emmental
    (Swiss) or Cheddar cheese, grated
salt and pepper
chopped fresh parsley to garnish

1 Heat the butter or margarine and oil in a saucepan, add the onions and garlic and fry very gently for 10–15 minutes until soft.

2 Increase the heat a little and continue to fry, stirring frequently, until the onions turn a golden brown and become caramelized.

3 Add the bay leaves, sugar, vinegar, seasoning and allspice. Add the stock and bring to the boil. Cover the pan and simmer gently for about 30 minutes.

4 Discard the bay leaves and adjust the seasoning. At this stage the soup may be cooled and chilled for up to 48 hours, or frozen for up to 6 weeks.

5 Toast 1 side of each slice of French bread under a preheated grill (broiler). Turn the slices over and sprinkle with the cheese. Put under the grill (broiler) until the cheese is bubbling.

6 Reheat the soup. Carefully ladle the soup into warmed soup bowls and float 2 slices of toasted bread on each portion. Sprinkle with chopped parsley. Allow the bread to soak up the soup a little and serve.

CARAMELIZING

Cooking the onions slowly and gently is vital to the success of this soup. It allows the natural sugars in the onions to caramelize, which gives the soup its characteristic rich flavour and colour.

STEP 1

STEP 2

STEP 5

STEP 6

BEETROOT SOUPS

Here are two variations using the same vegetable: Creamed Beetroot Soup (shown right) made with puréed cooked beetroot; and a traditional Bortsch, which is a clear soup finished with a swirl of soured cream.

SERVES 4–6

BORTSCH:
500 g/1 lb raw beetroot, peeled and grated
2 carrots, chopped finely
1 large onion, chopped finely
1 garlic clove, crushed
1 Bouquet Garni (see page 78)
1 litre/1¾ pints /4 cups Chicken or
    Vegetable Stock (see pages 77–8)
2–3 tsp lemon juice
salt and pepper
150 ml/¼ pint/⅔ cup soured cream to
    serve

CREAMED BEETROOT SOUP:
60 g/2 oz/¼ cup butter or margarine
2 large onions, chopped finely
1–2 carrots, chopped
2 celery sticks, chopped
500 g/1 lb cooked beetroot, diced
1–2 tbsp lemon juice
900 ml/1½ pints/3½ cups Chicken, Beef or
    Vegetable Stock (see pages 76–8)
300 ml/½ pint/1¼ cups milk
salt and pepper
grated cooked beetroot or 6 tbsp soured or
    double (heavy) cream, lightly whipped, to
    serve

1 To make bortsch, place the beetroot, carrots, onion, garlic, bouquet garni, stock, lemon juice and seasoning in a saucepan. Bring to the boil, cover and simmer for 45 minutes.

2 Pour the soup through a sieve (strainer) lined with muslin (cheesecloth) or a fine sieve (strainer), then pour into a clean pan. Adjust the seasoning and add extra lemon juice if necessary.

3 Bring to the boil and simmer for 1–2 minutes. Serve with a spoonful of soured cream swirled through.

4 To make creamed beetroot soup, melt the butter or margarine in a saucepan and fry the onions, carrots and celery until just beginning to colour.

5 Add the beetroot, 1 tablespoon of the lemon juice, the stock and seasoning and bring to the boil. Cover and simmer for 30 minutes until tender.

6 Cool slightly, then press through a sieve (strainer) or blend in a food processor or blender. Pour into a clean pan. Add the milk and bring to the boil. Adjust the seasoning, add extra lemon juice if necessary, topped with grated beetroot or cream and serve.

STEP 1

STEP 3

STEP 4

STEP 6

CREAMED PARSNIP & TARRAGON SOUP

The creamy texture and subtle flavouring of this soup will make it a favourite with everyone, for everyday meals or special occasions.

SERVES 4–6

1 carrot
500 g/ 1 lb parsnips
45 g/ 1¹/₂ oz/ 3 tbsp butter or margarine
1 large onion, chopped
1 garlic clove, crushed (optional)
900 ml/ 1¹/₂ pints/ 3¹/₂ cups Chicken or
    Vegetable Stock (see pages 77–8)
2 tbsp lemon juice
2–3 sprigs fresh tarragon or 2 tsp dried
    tarragon
300 ml/ ¹/₂ pint/ 1¹/₄ cups milk
150 ml/ ¹/₄ pint/ ²/₃ cup natural fromage frais
    or single (light) cream
2 tsp chopped fresh tarragon
salt and pepper
Fried Croûtons (see page 79) to serve

1 Peel the carrot and slice. Peel the parsnips and cut into chunks.

2 Melt the butter or margarine in a large saucepan and fry the onion and garlic, if using, until soft but not coloured.

3 Add the parsnips and carrot and continue to fry for a few minutes, tossing the vegetables and stirring frequently. Add the stock and bring to the boil.

4 Add the seasoning, lemon juice and tarragon, cover and simmer for about 30 minutes until the vegetables are very tender.

5 Discard the fresh tarragon sprigs, if using, cool the soup a little, then press through a sieve (strainer) or blend in a food processor or blender until smooth.

6 Pour into a clean saucepan and add the milk. Bring slowly to the boil. Beat the fromage frais, if using, until smooth and add this or the cream to the soup and reheat again gently, but do not allow to boil. Adjust the seasoning and stir in half the chopped tarragon. Serve the soup with the fried croutons and the remaining tarragon sprinkled on top.

FREEZING

This soup can be frozen for up to 3 months. Add the fromage frais or cream when reheating.

CREAMED CARROT & CUMIN SOUP

Carrot soups are very popular and are always an attractive colour.
Flavourings can vary widely but here cumin, tomato, potato and celery
give the soup both richness and depth.

STEP 2

STEP 3

STEP 4

STEP 5

SERVES 4–6

45 g/ 1½ oz/ 3 tbsp butter or margarine
1 large onion, chopped
1–2 garlic cloves, crushed
350 g/ 12 oz carrots, sliced
900 ml/ 1½ pints/ 3½ cups Chicken or
    Vegetable Stock (see pages 77–8)
¾ tsp ground cumin
2 celery sticks, sliced thinly
125 g/ 4 oz potato, diced
2 tsp tomato purée (paste)
2 tsp lemon juice
2 fresh or dried bay leaves
about 300 ml/ ½ pint/ 1¼ cups milk
salt and pepper
celery leaves to garnish

1 Melt the butter or margarine in a large saucepan. Add the onion and garlic and fry very gently until the onion begins to soften.

2 Add the carrots and continue to fry gently for a further 5 minutes, stirring frequently and taking care they do not brown.

3 Add the stock, cumin, seasoning, celery, potato, tomato purée (paste), lemon juice and bay leaves and bring to the boil. Cover and simmer

gently for about 30 minutes until all the vegetables are very tender.

4 Discard the bay leaves, cool the soup a little and then press it through a sieve (strainer) or blend in a food processor or blender until smooth.

5 Pour the soup into a clean pan, add the milk and bring slowly to the boil. Taste and adjust the seasoning.

6 Garnish each serving with a small celery leaf and serve.

FREEZING

This soup can be frozen for up to 3 months. Add the milk when reheating.

CREAM OF ARTICHOKE SOUP

A creamy soup with the unique, subtle flavouring of Jerusalem artichokes and a garnish of grated carrots for extra crunch. This is thought by many to be the very best of the vegetable soups.

STEP 1

STEP 2

STEP 4

STEP 6

SERVES 4–6

1.25 litres/ 2¼ pints/ 5 cups Chicken or
  Vegetable Stock (see pages 77–8)
750 g/ 1½ lb Jerusalem artichokes
1 lemon, sliced thickly
60 g/ 2 oz/¼ cup butter or margarine
2 onions, chopped
1 garlic clove, crushed
2 bay leaves, preferably fresh
¼ tsp ground mace or ground nutmeg
1 tbsp lemon juice
150 ml/¼ pint/⅔ cup single (light) cream
  or natural fromage frais
salt and pepper

TO GARNISH:
coarsely grated carrot
chopped fresh parsley or coriander (cilantro)

1 Make the stock, if necessary (see pages 77–8).

2 Peel and slice the artichokes. Put into a bowl of water with the lemon slices.

3 Melt the butter or margarine in a large saucepan. Add the onions and garlic and fry gently for 3–4 minutes until soft but not coloured.

4 Drain the artichokes and add to the pan. Mix well and cook gently for 2–3 minutes without allowing to colour.

5 Add the stock, seasoning, bay leaves, mace or nutmeg and lemon juice and bring slowly to the boil. Cover and simmer gently for about 30 minutes until the vegetables are very tender.

6 Discard the bay leaves, cool slightly then press through a sieve (strainer) or blend the soup in a food processor or blender until smooth. If liked, a little of the soup may be only partially pureed and added to the rest of the pureed soup, to give extra texture.

7 Pour into a clean pan and bring to the boil. Adjust the seasoning and stir in the cream or fromage frais. Reheat gently without boiling. Garnish with grated carrot and chopped parsley or coriander (cilantro) and serve.

FREEZING

This soup can be frozen for up to 3 months. Add the cream or fromage frais when reheating.

STEP 1

STEP 3

STEP 5

STEP 6

PUMPKIN SOUP

This is an American classic that has now become popular worldwide. With its subtle flavour and attractive orange colour, it will soon become a firm favourite with you, too. When pumpkin is out of season use butternut squash in its place.

SERVES 4–6

about 1 kg/2 lb pumpkin
45 g/1¹/₂ oz/3 tbsp butter or margarine
1 onion, sliced thinly
1 garlic clove, crushed
900 ml/1¹/₂ pints/3¹/₂ cups Chicken or
    Vegetable Stock (see pages 77–8)
¹/₂ tsp ground ginger
1 tbsp lemon juice
3–4 thinly pared strips of orange rind
    (optional)
1–2 fresh or dried bay leaves or 1 Bouquet
    Garni (see page 78)
300 ml/¹/₂ pint/1¹/₄ cups milk
salt and pepper

TO GARNISH:
4–6 tablespoons single (light) or double
    (heavy) cream, natural yogurt or fromage
    frais
snipped chives

1 Peel the pumpkin, remove the seeds and then cut the flesh into 2.5 cm/1 inch cubes.

2 Melt the butter or margarine in a large saucepan, add the onion and garlic and fry gently until soft but not coloured.

3 Add the pumpkin and toss with the onion for a few minutes.

4 Add the stock and bring to the boil. Add the seasoning, ginger, lemon juice, strips of orange rind, if using, and bay leaves or bouquet garni, cover and simmer gently for about 20 minutes until the pumpkin is very tender.

5 Discard the orange rind, if using, and the bay leaves or bouquet garni. Cool the soup a little and then press through a sieve (strainer) or blend in a food processor or blender until smooth. Pour into a clean saucepan.

6 Add the milk and reheat gently. Adjust the seasoning. Garnish with a swirl of cream, natural yogurt or fromage frais and snipped chives and serve.

PUMPKINS

Pumpkins are usually sold whole but if they are very large you may be able to buy just a half or a quarter.

STEP 2

STEP 3

STEP 5

STEP 6

GARDENER'S BROTH

This thick, hearty soup uses a variety of green vegetables with a flavouring of ground coriander. A finishing touch of thinly sliced leeks adds texture.

SERVES 4–6

45 g/ 1 1/2 oz/ 3 tbsp butter or margarine
1 onion, chopped
1–2 garlic cloves, crushed
1 large leek
250 g/8 oz Brussels sprouts
125 g/4 oz French (green) or runner beans
1.25 litres/ 2 1/4 pints/ 5 cups Vegetable or
  Chicken Stock (see pages 77–8)
125 g/4 oz/ 3/4 cup frozen peas
1 tbsp lemon juice
1/2 tsp ground coriander
4 tbsp double (heavy) cream
salt and pepper

MELBA TOAST:
4–6 slices white bread

1 Melt the butter or margarine in a saucepan, add the onion and garlic and fry very gently, stirring occasionally, until they begin to soften but not colour.

2 Slice the white part of the leek very thinly and reserve; slice the remaining leeks. Slice the Brussels sprouts and thinly slice the beans.

3 Add the green part of the leeks, the Brussels sprouts and beans to the saucepan. Add the stock and bring to the boil. Simmer for 10 minutes. Add the frozen peas, seasoning, lemon juice and coriander and continue to simmer for 10–15 minutes until the vegetables are tender.

4 Cool the soup a little, then press through a sieve (strainer) or blend in a food processor or blender until smooth. Pour into a clean pan.

5 Add the reserved slices of leek to the soup, bring back to the boil and simmer for about 5 minutes until the leeks are tender. Adjust the seasoning, stir in the cream and reheat gently.

6 Make the melba toast. Toast the bread on both sides under a preheated grill (broiler). Cut horizontally through the slices then toast the uncooked sides until they curl up. Serve immediately with the soup.

FREEZING

This soup can be frozen for up to 2 months. Add the cream when reheating.

CHAPTER THREE

Fish Soups

Fish soups are particularly popular and can be made with a huge variety of fish and shellfish. Many are so full of fish that they need a fork as well as a spoon to eat them. They often include shellfish such as mussels and prawns (shrimp), so a bowl for the discarded 'debris' is often required on the table, plus a finger bowl and napkin for cleaning up afterwards!

As with most soups, the basis of a good fish soup is a good stock. It may seem a bit of trouble to make Fish Stock (see page 77), but it is often possible to buy fish heads and trimmings which are ideal for home-made stock, and it is much quicker to make than other stocks — it only needs 30 minutes of simmering. But if you don't have the time, some supermarkets sell fresh fish stock and there are now good fish stock cubes available, both of which can be used as alternatives. Chicken or vegetable stock can also be used.

It is best to make soups from fresh fish. Although specialist fishmongers are becoming more rare, they can often be found in markets, and many larger supermarkets now have an impressive wet fish counter. Frozen fish can be used if necessary, but if you want to freeze the soup, make sure the fish has been well cooked.

Opposite: *Shellfish such as mussels and prawns (shrimp) do not keep well and should be prepared and cooked as soon as possible after buying.*

BOUILLABAISSE

This famous French soup is traditionally made from at least eight varieties of fish and shellfish. Many of those used are only available from the Mediterranean, but you should be able to get a good enough selection from your fishmonger or supermarket.

STEP 1

STEP 3

STEP 4

STEP 6

SERVES 4–6

750 g–1 kg/ 1½–2 lb mixed fish and
  shellfish such as whiting, mackerel, red or
  grey mullet, cod, eel, bass, crab, prawns
  (shrimp), lobster, squid and mussels
2 large onions, sliced thinly or chopped
2 celery sticks, sliced very thinly
1 carrot, chopped finely
2–3 garlic cloves, crushed
4 tbsp olive oil
425 g/14 oz can chopped tomatoes with
  mixed herbs or 350 g/12 oz fresh
  tomatoes, skinned and chopped
1 fresh or dried bay leaf
¼ tsp ground coriander
few sprigs of fresh mixed herbs, including
  parsley
1 tsp grated lemon rind
1–2 tbsp lemon juice
about 300 ml/½ pint/ 1¼ cups water
pinch of saffron threads or ground turmeric
salt and pepper
chopped mixed herbs to garnish

1 Clean the fish, removing any skin and bones, and cut into pieces about 5 x 2.5 cm/2 x 1 inches. Remove the heads from the prawns (shrimp). Cut the squid into rings. Scrub the mussels.

2 Gently fry the onions, celery, carrot and garlic in the oil in a large saucepan for about 5 minutes until soft but not coloured.

3 Stir in the tomatoes, bay leaf, coriander, herbs, seasoning and lemon rind and juice.

4 Arrange all the fish and shellfish in the pan over the vegetables.

5 Put the measured water in another saucepan, add the saffron or turmeric and bring to the boil. Pour into the saucepan of fish, adding enough to just cover the fish.

6 Bring to the boil, cover and simmer for about 20 minutes until the fish is tender but not broken up.

7 Discard the bay leaf and herbs, then ladle the soup into bowls, sprinkle with the chopped mixed herbs and serve. Both a soup spoon and fork are needed to eat this soup.

STEP 1

STEP 3

STEP 4

STEP 5

MOULES MARINIERE

A true French soup of mussels cooked in white wine with onions, garlic, herbs and cream. It can be served as an appetizer or a main dish, with plenty of warm crusty bread.

SERVES 4

about 3 litres/ 5 pints/ 12 cups fresh mussels
60 g/ 2 oz/ ¼ cup butter
1 large onion, chopped very finely
2–3 garlic cloves, crushed
350 ml/ 12 fl oz/ 1½ cups dry white wine
150 ml/ ¼ pint/ ⅔ cup water
2 tbsp lemon juice
good pinch of finely grated lemon rind
1 Bouquet Garni (see page 78)
1 tbsp plain (all-purpose) flour
4 tbsp single (light) or double (thick) cream
2–3 tbsp chopped fresh parsley
salt and pepper
warm crusty bread to serve

1 Scrub the mussels in several changes of cold water to remove all mud, sand, barnacles, etc. Pull off all the 'beards'. All the mussels must be tightly closed; if they don't close when given a sharp tap, they must be discarded.

2 Melt half the butter in a large saucepan. Add the onion and garlic and fry gently until soft but not coloured.

3 Add the wine, water, lemon juice and rind, bouquet garni and plenty of seasoning and bring to the boil. Cover and simmer for 4–5 minutes.

4 Add the mussels to the pan, cover tightly and simmer for 5 minutes, shaking the pan frequently, until all the mussels have opened. Discard any mussels which have not opened and remove the bouquet garni.

5 Remove the mussels from the pan and take the empty half shell off each one. Blend the remaining butter with the flour and whisk into the soup, a little at a time. Simmer gently for 2–3 minutes until slightly thickened.

6 Add the cream and half the parsley to the soup and reheat gently. Adjust the seasoning. Ladle the mussels and soup into warmed large soup bowls, sprinkle with the remaining parsley and serve with plenty of warm crusty bread.

MUSSELS

Before cooking mussels it is important to discard any that are not closed, as they are dead. Similarly, be sure to discard any which do not open during cooking.

PARTAN BREE

This traditional Scottish soup is thickened with a purée of rice and crab meat cooked in milk. Extra crab meat is added with fresh herbs and a little soured cream, if liked, at the end of cooking.

STEP 1

SERVES 4–6

1 medium-sized boiled crab
90 g/ 3 oz/ scant ½ cup long-grain rice
600 ml/ 1 pint/ 2½ cups milk
600 ml/ 1 pint/ 2½ cups Fish Stock (see page 77)
1 tbsp anchovy essence
2 tsp lime or lemon juice
1 tbsp chopped fresh parsley or 1 tsp chopped fresh thyme
3–4 tbsp soured cream (optional)
salt and pepper
snipped chives to garnish

1 Remove and reserve all the brown and white meat from the crab, then crack the claws and remove and chop that meat; reserve the claw meat.

2 Put the rice and milk into a saucepan and bring slowly to the boil. Cover and simmer gently for about 20 minutes until the rice is very tender.

3 Add the reserved white and brown crab meat and seasoning and simmer for a further 5 minutes.

4 Cool a little, then press through a sieve (strainer), or blend in a food processor or blender until smooth.

5 Pour the soup into a clean saucepan and add the fish stock and the reserved claw meat. Bring slowly to the boil, then add the anchovy essence and lime or lemon juice and adjust the seasoning.

6 Simmer for a further 2–3 minutes. Stir in the parsley or thyme and then swirl soured cream, if using, through each serving. Garnish with snipped chives.

STEP 3

STEP 5

CRAB

Cooked crabs are readily available from fishmongers and larger supermarkets that have a fish counter. They are also available frozen from some shops. If you are unable to buy a whole crab, use about 175 g/6 oz frozen crab meat, which must be thoroughly thawed before use; or a 175 g/6 oz can of crab meat which just needs thorough draining and flaking before use.

STEP 6

PRAWN (SHRIMP) GUMBO

This soup is thick with onions, red (bell) peppers, rice, prawns (shrimp) and okra, which both adds flavour and acts as a thickening agent.

STEP 1

STEP 2

STEP 3

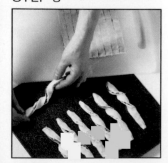

STEP 4

SERVES 4–6

1 large onion, chopped finely
2 slices lean bacon, chopped finely (optional)
1–2 garlic cloves, crushed
2 tbsp olive oil
1 large or 2 small red (bell) peppers,
    chopped finely or minced coarsely
900 ml/ 1¹/₂ pints/ 3¹/₂ cups Fish or
    Vegetable Stock (see pages 77–8)
1 fresh or dried bay leaf
1 blade mace
good pinch of ground allspice
45 g/ 1¹/₂ oz/ 3 tbsp long-grain rice
1 tbsp white wine vinegar
125–175 g/ 4–6 oz okra, trimmed and
    sliced very thinly
90–125 g/ 3–4 oz/ ¹/₂–²/₃ cup peeled prawns
    (shrimp)
1 tbsp anchovy essence (paste)
2 tsp tomato purée (paste)
1–2 tbsp chopped fresh parsley
salt and pepper
Cheese & Anchovy Twists (see page 79) to
    serve

TO GARNISH:
whole prawns (shrimp)
sprigs of fresh parsley

1 Gently fry the onion, bacon, if using, and garlic in the oil in a large saucepan for 4–5 minutes until soft, but only lightly coloured. Add the (bell) peppers to the pan and continue to fry gently for a couple of minutes.

2 Add the stock, bay leaf, mace, allspice, rice, vinegar and seasoning and bring to the boil. Cover and simmer gently for about 20 minutes, giving an occasional stir, until the rice is just tender.

3 Add the okra, prawns (shrimp), anchovy essence (paste) and tomato purée (paste), cover and simmer gently for about 15 minutes until the okra is tender and the mixture slightly thickened.

4 Meanwhile, make the cheese and anchovy twists (see page 79).

5 Discard the bay leaf and mace from the soup and adjust the seasoning. Stir in the parsley and serve each portion garnished with a whole prawn (shrimp) and parsley sprigs. Serve with warm cheese and anchovy twists.

STEP 2

STEP 3

STEP 5

STEP 6

SMOKY HADDOCK SOUP

Smoked haddock gives this soup a good rich flavour, while mashed potatoes and cream thicken and enrich the stock.

SERVES 4–6

250 g / 8 oz smoked haddock fillet
1 onion, chopped finely
1 garlic clove, crushed
600 ml / 1 pint / 2½ cups water
600 ml / 1 pint / 2½ cups milk
250–350 g / 8–12 oz / 1–1½ cups hot
  mashed potatoes
30 g / 1 oz / 2 tbsp butter
about 1 tbsp lemon juice
6 tbsp double (heavy) cream, soured cream
  or natural fromage frais
4 tbsp chopped fresh parsley
salt and pepper

1 Put the fish, onion, garlic and water into a saucepan. Bring to the boil, cover and simmer gently for about 15–20 minutes until the fish is tender.

2 Remove the fish from the pan; strip off the skin and remove all the bones. Flake the flesh finely.

3 Return the skin and bones to the cooking liquor and simmer for 10 minutes. Strain, discarding the skin and bones, and pour the liquor into a clean saucepan.

4 Add the milk, flaked fish and seasoning to the pan, bring to the boil and simmer for about 3 minutes.

5 Gradually whisk in sufficient mashed potato to give a fairly thick soup, then stir in the butter and sharpen to taste with lemon juice.

6 Add the cream, soured cream or fromage frais and 3 tablespoons of the chopped parsley. Reheat gently and adjust the seasoning. Sprinkle with the remaining parsley and serve.

SMOKED HADDOCK

Undyed smoked haddock may be used in place of the bright yellow fish; it will give a paler colour but just as much flavour. Alternatively, use smoked cod or smoked whiting.

STEP 1

STEP 3

STEP 5

STEP 6

SALMON BISQUE

A filling soup which is ideal for all types of occasion, from an elegant dinner to a picnic. It can be made from salmon heads or pieces and, for a touch of luxury, garnished with smoked salmon.

SERVES 4–6

*1–2 salmon heads (depending on size) or a
   tail piece of salmon weighing about
   500 g/1 lb
900 ml/1½ pints/3½ cups water
1 fresh or dried bay leaf
1 lemon, sliced
a few black peppercorns
30 g/1 oz/2 tbsp butter or margarine
2 tbsp finely chopped onion or spring onions
   (scallions)
30 g/1 oz/¼ cup plain (all-purpose) flour
150 ml/¼ pint /²/₃ cup dry white wine or
   Fish Stock (see page 77)
150 ml/¼ pint/²/₃ cup single (light) cream
1 tbsp chopped fresh fennel or dill
2–3 tsp lemon or lime juice
salt and pepper*

*TO GARNISH:
30–45 g/1–1½ oz smoked salmon pieces,
   chopped (optional)
sprigs of fresh fennel or dill*

1 Put the salmon, water, bay leaf, lemon and peppercorns into a saucepan. Bring to the boil, remove any scum from the surface, then cover the pan and simmer gently for 20 minutes.

2 Remove from the heat, strain the stock and reserve 600 ml/1 pint/ 2½ cups.

3 Remove and discard all the skin and bones from the salmon and flake the flesh, removing all the pieces from the head, if using.

4 Melt the butter or margarine in a saucepan and fry the onion or spring onions (scallions) gently for about 5 minutes until soft. Stir in the flour and cook for 1 minute then gradually stir in the reserved stock and wine or fish stock. Bring to the boil, stirring.

5 Add the salmon, season well, then simmer gently for about 5 minutes.

6 Add the cream and the chopped fennel or dill and reheat gently, but do not boil. Sharpen to taste with lemon or lime juice and adjust the seasoning. Serve hot or chilled, garnished with smoked salmon, if using, and sprigs of fennel or dill.

CHAPTER FOUR

Chowders

A chowder is a thick and chunky soup, full of chopped vegetables, meat, fish, shellfish, pasta or rice, to suit meat-eaters and vegetarians alike. Hearty and filling, it is usually served as a snack or a meal in itself, rather than as a first course.

It is again important to use a well flavoured stock as the base for a chowder. The thickening agent may be a roux, a beurre manié, or a blend of egg yolks and cream (see page 79). Rice, barley, potatoes, or a purée of some of the soup also thicken a chowder.

Chowders are an excellent way to use up leftovers, whether meat, fish or vegetables. Vegetables are used in many forms: they may be finely chopped or diced, thinly sliced, cut into thin strips or coarsely grated. A food processor is a useful piece of equipment for preparing the vegetables in the minimum of time. If raw meat is added, it should be minced (ground) and added at the start of cooking. Raw poultry and fish need only be chopped, but again added early on. Cooked meats, poultry and fish can be added part way through cooking but also need to be chopped or minced (ground).

Opposite: *Chunky vegetables are an important part of a chowder. Make sure you cut them into even-sized pieces so they cook evenly.*

STEP 2

STEP 3

STEP 4

STEP 5

HOLLANDAISE OATMEAL CHOWDER

An unusual soup made with chunky vegetables and oatmeal and given a little bite by adding vinegar and mayonnaise. Oatcakes are the ideal accompaniment.

SERVES 4–6

60 g/2 oz/¼ cup butter or margarine
2 large onions, chopped finely or sliced very thinly
1 garlic clove, crushed
1 turnip
3 carrots
3 celery sticks and/or 175 g/6 oz celeriac (celery root)
1 leek
45 g/1½ oz/½ cup medium oatmeal
1 litre/1¾ pints/4 cups stock
150 ml/¼ pint/⅔ cup milk
about 2 tbsp white wine vinegar
1 egg yolk
150 ml/¼ pint/⅔ cup single (light) cream
2 tbsp mayonnaise
salt and pepper
chopped fresh herbs and herb sprigs to garnish
oatcakes to serve

1 Melt the butter or margarine in a saucepan and gently fry the onions and garlic for about 10 minutes until very soft but not coloured.

2 Finely chop the turnip, carrots and celery and/or celeriac (celery root). Thinly slice the leek.

3 Add the vegetables to the pan and continue to fry, stirring from time to time, for about 5 minutes. Add the oatmeal and cook for a further minute.

4 Add the stock and then the milk and bring to the boil. Season well, add 2 tablespoons of vinegar, cover and simmer for about 30 minutes until the vegetables are very tender.

5 Mix the egg yolk with the cream, add a little of the soup to the cream and then whisk it all back into the soup, followed by the mayonnaise.

6 Bring slowly back just to the boil, adjust the seasoning and add extra vinegar, if necessary, to sharpen the taste. Garnish with herbs and serve with oatcakes.

VARIATION

This soup can be varied by adding 90–125 g/3–4 oz/¾–1 cup crumbled blue cheese in place of the cream and egg yolk, and adding an extra 150 ml/¼ pint/⅔ cup milk or stock in place of the cream.

CURRIED COD CHOWDER

Chunks of white fish cooked with root vegetables and rice and flavoured with tomatoes and curry powder.

STEP 2

STEP 3

STEP 4

STEP 5

SERVES 4–6

30 g/1 oz/2 tbsp butter or margarine
1 tbsp olive oil
1 onion, chopped finely
2 celery sticks, chopped finely
1 garlic clove, crushed
1¹/₂ tsp medium curry powder
700 ml/1¹/₄ pints/3 cups Fish or Vegetable
   Stock (see pages 77–8)
1 fresh or dried bay leaf
350 g/12 oz haddock or cod fillet, skinned
   and chopped coarsely
425 g/14 oz can chopped tomatoes
1 tbsp tomato purée (paste)
60 g/2 oz/¹/₄ cup long-grain rice
1 carrot, grated coarsely
2 tsp lemon juice
4 tbsp single (light) or double (heavy) cream
   or natural fromage frais
2 tsp chopped fresh mixed herbs
salt and pepper
crusty bread to serve

1 Melt the butter or margarine with the oil in a saucepan, add the onion, celery and garlic and gently fry until soft but not coloured.

2 Stir in the curry powder, cook for 1 minute and then add the stock, bay leaf and seasoning. Bring to the boil.

3 Add the fish, cover and simmer gently for about 10 minutes until the flesh flakes easily.

4 Break up the fish, then add the tomatoes, tomato purée (paste), rice, carrot and lemon juice. Bring back to the boil, cover and simmer for 20 minutes until the rice is tender.

5 Stir in the cream or fromage frais and the herbs and adjust the seasoning. Reheat and serve with plenty of crusty bread.

VARIATION

Prawns (shrimp), smoked fish or salmon, or a mixture of fish may also be used for this chowder.

COCK-A-LEEKIE SOUP

A traditional Scottish soup in which a whole chicken is cooked with the vegetables to add extra flavour to the stock. Add some of the cooked chicken to the soup and reserve the remainder for another meal.

STEP 1

SERVES 4–6

1–1.5 kg/2–3 lb oven-ready chicken plus giblets, if available
1.75 – 2 litres/3–3½ pints/8–9 cups Chicken Stock (see page 77)
1 onion, sliced
4 leeks, sliced thinly
good pinch of ground allspice or ground coriander
1 Bouquet Garni (see page 78)
12 no-need-to-soak prunes, halved and pitted
salt and pepper
warm crusty bread to serve

1 Put the chicken, giblets, if using, stock and onion in a large saucepan.

2 Bring to the boil and remove any scum from the surface.

3 Add the leeks, seasoning, allspice or coriander and bouquet garni to the pan, cover and simmer gently for about 1½ hours until the chicken is falling off the bones.

4 Remove the chicken and bouquet garni from the pan and skim any fat from the surface of the soup.

5 Chop some of the chicken flesh and return to the pan. Add the prunes, bring back to the boil and simmer, uncovered, for about 20 minutes.

6 Adjust the seasoning and serve with warm crusty bread.

STEP 3

STEP 4

CHICKEN STOCK

You can replace the chicken stock with 3 chicken stock cubes dissolved in the same amount of water, if you prefer.

STEP 5

STEP 1

STEP 2

STEP 3

STEP 4

SAGE & ONION CHOWDER

A thick, creamy onion soup full of chopped bacon, potatoes and sweetcorn with plenty of fragrant fresh sage.

SERVES 4–6

60 g/ 2 oz/ $^1/_4$ cup butter or margarine
4 onions, sliced very thinly or chopped
1–2 garlic cloves, crushed
4 slices lean bacon, chopped
2 tbsp plain (all-purpose) flour
900 ml/ 1 $^1/_2$ pints/ 3 $^1/_2$ cups Chicken or Vegetable Stock (see pages 77–8)
500 g/ 1 lb potatoes, diced very finely
300 ml/ $^1/_2$ pint/ $^2/_3$ cup creamy milk
about 200 g/ 7 oz can sweetcorn, well drained
1 tbsp chopped fresh sage or 1 $^1/_2$ tsp dried sage
2 tbsp white wine vinegar
salt and pepper
sprigs of fresh sage to garnish
Cheese Scones (see pages 77–8), warmed, to serve

1 Melt the butter or margarine in a large saucepan and fry the onions and garlic very gently for about 15 minutes until soft but not coloured.

2 Add the bacon and continue to fry for a few minutes, allowing the onions to colour a little. Stir in the flour and cook for a further minute or so.

3 Add the stock, bring to the boil, then add the potatoes and seasoning and simmer gently for 20 minutes.

4 Add the milk and sweetcorn and bring back to the boil, then add the sage and vinegar and simmer for a further 10–15 minutes until the potatoes are very tender but not broken up.

5 Adjust the seasoning, garnish with sprigs of sage and serve with warmed cheese scones.

VARIATION

Frozen sweetcorn can be used instead of the canned variety. Add to the soup in step 4 — there's no need to thaw it first.

RED BEAN CHOWDER

A real hearty chowder full of mixed chopped vegetables and minced (ground) beef and spiced with chilli powder. This recipe uses dried beans but if you're short of time, you can used canned beans instead.

STEP 1

STEP 3

STEP 4

STEP 5

SERVES 4–6

175 g/6 oz/1 cup dried red kidney beans, soaked overnight and drained or 425 g/ 14 oz can red kidney beans, drained
900 ml/1½ pints/3½ cups water if using dried beans
45 g/1½ oz/3 tbsp butter or margarine
1 large onion, chopped very finely
1 large carrot, chopped finely
1–2 celery sticks, chopped finely
1 small turnip, chopped finely
2 garlic cloves, crushed
175 g/6 oz/¾ cup extra lean finely minced (ground) beef
2 tbsp plain (all-purpose) flour
1–2 tsp chilli powder
900 ml/1½ pints/3½ cups Beef Stock (see page 77)
2 tsp tomato purée (paste)
4 tomatoes, skinned and chopped finely
1 tsp chopped fresh oregano or ½ tsp dried oregano
salt and pepper

1 If using dried kidney beans, put them in a saucepan with the water, bring to the boil and boil hard for 10–15 minutes, reduce the heat and simmer for about 1–1½ hours until tender; drain.

2 Melt the butter or margarine in a saucepan and fry the onion, carrot, celery, turnip and garlic very slowly for about 10 minutes until soft.

3 Add the beef and cook slowly, stirring frequently, for 10 minutes until cooked and lightly browned.

4 Stir in the flour and chilli powder and cook for 2 minutes. Gradually stir in the stock and tomato purée (paste) and bring to the boil, stirring.

5 Season the chowder, cover the pan and simmer for 30 minutes. Stir in the tomatoes, oregano and beans.

6 Return to the boil and simmer for 5 minutes. If the soup seems very thick add a little more boiling water or stock. Adjust the seasoning and serve.

DRIED RED KIDNEY BEANS

If using dried red kidney beans it is essential that they are boiled hard for at least 10 minutes to kill any toxins; they may then be simmered gently until tender.

CHAPTER FIVE

Meat & Poultry Soups

Meat soups and broths are all based on some type of meat stock, be it made from beef bones, a poultry carcass, game, or a ham bone, and it is important that the stock is strongly flavoured. It is essential not to add too much extra meat to the soup, however, as the texture may be spoilt and the soup may be too thick and heavy.

Onions, garlic and a good bouquet garni or bay leaves are very important in these soups, and where herbs are called for, fresh ones will give a much better flavour. As dried herbs have a more intense flavour, you should roughly double the quantity if using fresh herbs. Fresh herbs also make attractive garnishes: float some leaves or sprigs on top of the soup just before serving or sprinkle with chopped herbs to add a splash of freshness and colour.

Opposite: Meat soups are an economical choice as the long slow cooking means you can use cheaper cuts of meat.

CHICKEN & CHESTNUT SOUP

A rich soup based on a good stock with pieces of chicken and chopped chestnuts for an interesting flavour and texture.

STEP 1

STEP 3

STEP 4

STEP 5

SERVES 4–6

2 onions
raw or cooked chicken carcass, chopped, plus
    trimmings
chicken giblets, if available
1.5 litres/2¹/₂ pints/6¹/₄ cups water
1 Bouquet Garni (see page 78)
125 g/4 oz/¹/₂ cup fresh chestnuts, pierced
    and roasted for about 5 minutes or boiled
    for 30–40 minutes, drained, or 175 g/
    6 oz/1 cup canned peeled chestnuts
45 g/1¹/₂ oz/3 tbsp butter or margarine
45 g/1¹/₂ oz/¹/₃ cup plain (all-purpose) flour
150 ml/¹/₄ pint/²/₃ cup milk
¹/₂ tsp ground coriander
90 g/3 oz/1¹/₂ cups carrots, grated coarsely
1 tbsp chopped fresh parsley (optional)
salt and pepper

1 Cut 1 of the onions into quarters. Put the chicken carcass, giblets, if available, water, the quartered onion and bouquet garni into a saucepan. Bring to the boil, cover and simmer for about 1 hour, giving an occasional stir.

2 Strain the stock and reserve 1 litre/1¾ pints/4 cups.

3 Remove 90–125 g/3–4 oz/¹/₂–¾ cup of chicken trimmings from the carcass and chop finely. If using fresh chestnuts, peel them; if using canned ones, drain well. Finely chop the chestnuts. Chop the remaining onion.

4 Melt the butter or margarine in a saucepan and fry the onion gently until soft. Stir in the flour and cook for a minute or so. Gradually stir in the reserved stock and bring to the boil, stirring.

5 Simmer for 2 minutes, then add the milk, seasoning, coriander, chopped chicken, carrots and chestnuts.

6 Bring back to the boil and simmer for 10 minutes, then stir in the parsley, if using. Adjust the seasoning and serve.

CHICKEN CARCASS

For this soup, use a carcass that still has a certain amount of meat left on the bones. Otherwise use 1–2 chicken portions and 2–3 chicken stock cubes.

CREAMED PHEASANT SOUP

This is a rich, creamy soup flavoured with onion, garlic and mushrooms and is ideal for using up a leftover pheasant carcass. If you prefer, you can use a whole bird.

STEP 1

STEP 4

STEP 5

STEP 6

SERVES 4–6

1 raw or cooked pheasant carcass or 1 small
   oven-ready pheasant
1 onion, studded with 6 cloves
1.5 litres/2½ pints/6¼ cups water
60 g/2 oz/¼ cup butter or margarine
1 onion, chopped finely
45 g/1½ oz/⅓ cup plain (all-purpose) flour
½ tsp celery salt
¼ tsp ground coriander
30 g/1 oz/2 tbsp long-grain rice
125 g/4 oz/2 cups mushrooms, finely
   chopped
150 ml/¼ pint/⅔ cup single (light) or
   double (heavy) cream
2 tbsp chopped fresh parsley
salt and pepper
Fried Croûtons (see page 79) to serve

1 Put the pheasant carcass or the whole bird, the clove-studded onion and the water into a saucepan. Bring to the boil, cover and simmer for about 1½ hours. Drain off and reserve 1.25 litres/2¼ pints/5 cups of the stock. Remove about 90 g/3 oz/½ cup of meat from the carcass or from the leg or wing of the whole bird. Chop finely.

2 Melt the butter or margarine in a saucepan and fry the chopped onion gently for about 3 minutes until soft but not coloured.

3 Stir in the flour and cook for a minute or so, then gradually stir in the reserved stock and bring to the boil.

4 Add the seasoning, celery salt, coriander, rice and mushrooms, cover and simmer for about 20 minutes, stirring occasionally.

5 Add the reserved pheasant meat and the cream, adjust the seasoning and bring back just to the boil.

6 Just before serving stir in the parsley or, if preferred, stir in half the parsley and use the remainder to sprinkle over each serving. Serve with fried croûtons.

FREEZING

This soup can be frozen for up to 2 months. Add the cream and parsley when reheating.

STEP 1

STEP 2

STEP 4

STEP 4

CONSOMME

A traditional clear soup made from beef bones and lean minced (ground) beef. Thin strips of vegetables provide a colourful garnish.

SERVES 4–6

*1.25 litres/2¼ pints/5 cups strong Beef
    Stock (see page 77)
250 g/8 oz/1 cup extra lean minced
    (ground) beef
2 tomatoes, skinned, seeded and chopped
2 large carrots, chopped
1 large onion, chopped
2 celery sticks, chopped
1 turnip, chopped (optional)
1 Bouquet Garni (see page 78)
2–3 egg whites
shells of 2–4 eggs, crushed
1–2 tbsp sherry (optional)
salt and pepper
Melba Toast (see page 32) to serve*

*TO GARNISH:
julienne strips of raw carrot, turnip, celery
    or celeriac (celery root) or a one-egg
    omelette, cut into julienne strips*

1 Make the stock, if necessary (see page 76). Put the stock and minced (ground) beef in a saucepan and leave to stand for 1 hour.

2 Add the tomatoes, carrots, onion, celery, turnip, if using, bouquet garni, 2 of the egg whites, the crushed shells of 2 of the eggs and plenty of seasoning. Bring to almost boiling point, whisking hard all the time with a flat whisk.

3 Cover and simmer for 1 hour, taking care not to allow the layer of froth on top of the soup to break.

4 Pour through a jelly bag or scalded fine cloth, keeping the froth back until the last, then pour again through the ingredients in the cloth into a clean pan. The resulting liquid should be clear.

5 If the soup is not quite clear, return it to the pan with another egg white and the crushed shells of 2 more eggs. Repeat the whisking process as before and then boil for 10 minutes; strain again.

6 Add the sherry to the soup and reheat gently.

7 Place the garnish in the base of warmed soup bowls and carefully pour in the soup. Serve with melba toast.

SCOTCH BROTH

This old favourite was originally made with a sheep's head but stewing lamb is now used. It is cooked slowly with a selection of root vegetables, pearl barley and parsley to provide a delicious broth. The lamb may be quite fatty so be sure to skim the surface well.

STEP 1

STEP 3

STEP 4

STEP 5

SERVES 6

750 g–1 kg/ 1½–2 lb stewing lamb on the bone
2 litres/ 3½ pints/ 9 cups water
2 fresh or dried bay leaves
250 g/ 8 oz/ 1¼ cups carrots, chopped finely
1 turnip, chopped
2 onions, chopped finely
2 leeks, sliced very thinly
125–250 g/ 4–8 oz potatoes, diced finely
60 g/ 2 oz/ ¼ cup pearl barley
salt and pepper
3 tbsp chopped fresh parsley to garnish

1 Trim the meat, removing any excess fat. Put in a large saucepan with the water and bring to the boil.

2 Remove any scum from the surface then add the bay leaves and plenty of seasoning. Cover and simmer gently for 1½ hours.

3 Add all the vegetables and the barley, stir and bring back to a gentle simmer. Cover the pan and simmer for 1 hour until the barley and vegetables are very soft.

4 Cool slightly then skim the fat from the surface. Remove the last of the fat by placing paper towels on the surface to absorb the fat.

5 Adjust the seasoning. Remove the lamb, strip the meat from the bones and return to the soup. Alternatively, the pieces of meat can be served still on the bone: put a piece of meat in each serving bowl and ladle over the soup (a fork will then be required to eat the soup).

6 Sprinkle the parsley over each portion and serve.

REMOVING THE FAT

If time allows, leave the soup to cool after step 3. It will then be easy to lift the solidified fat from the surface.

STEP 2

STEP 3

STEP 4

STEP 5

LENTIL & HAM SOUP

This is a good hearty soup, ideal for a cold winter's day. It is based on a stock made from a ham knuckle, with plenty of vegetables and red lentils to thicken it and add flavour.

SERVES 4–6

250 g/8 oz/1 cup red lentils
1.5 litres/2½ pints/6¼ cups stock or water
2 onions, chopped
1 garlic clove, crushed
2 large carrots, chopped
1 ham knuckle or 175 g/6 oz lean bacon, chopped
4 large tomatoes, skinned and chopped
2 fresh or dried bay leaves
250 g/8 oz potatoes, chopped
1 tbsp white wine vinegar
¼ tsp ground allspice
salt and pepper
chopped spring onions (scallions) or chopped fresh parsley to garnish

1 Put the lentils and stock or water in a saucepan and leave to soak for 1–2 hours.

2 Add the onions, garlic, carrots, ham knuckle or bacon, tomatoes, bay leaves and seasoning.

3 Bring to the boil, cover and simmer for about 1 hour until the lentils are tender.

4 Add the potatoes and continue to simmer for about 20 minutes until both the potatoes and ham knuckle are tender.

5 Discard the bay leaves. Remove the knuckle and chop about 125 g/ 4 oz/¾ cup of the meat and reserve. If liked, press half the soup through a sieve (strainer) or blend in a food processor or blender until smooth. Return to the pan with the rest of the soup.

6 Adjust the seasoning, add the vinegar and allspice and the reserved chopped ham. Simmer gently for a further 5–10 minutes. Serve sprinkled liberally with spring onions (scallions) or chopped parsley.

SMOOTH CONSISTENCY

For a smoother consistency, press all of the soup through a sieve (strainer) or blend in a food processor or blender in step 5, before adding the meat.

SPLIT PEA & HAM SOUP

Either yellow or green split peas can be used for this recipe but both types must be well washed and soaked overnight before use. Any sort of ham bone can be used, but a small knuckle is the most economical.

SERVES 6

300 g/ 10 oz/ 1 1/4 cups dried yellow split
    peas
1.75 litres/ 3 pints/ 7 1/2 cups water
2 onions, chopped finely
1 small turnip, chopped finely
2 carrots, chopped finely
2–4 celery sticks, chopped finely
1 ham knuckle
1 Bouquet Garni (see page 78)
1/2 tsp dried thyme
1/2 tsp ground ginger
1 tbsp white wine vinegar
salt and pepper

1 Thoroughly wash the dried peas under cold running water, then place in a bowl with half the water and leave to soak overnight.

2 Put the soaked peas and their liquor, the remaining water, the onions, turnip, carrots and celery into a large saucepan, then add the ham knuckle, bouquet garni, dried thyme and ginger. Bring slowly to the boil.

3 Remove any scum from the surface of the soup, cover the pan and simmer gently for 2–2 1/2 hours until the peas are very tender.

4 Remove the ham knuckle and bouquet garni. Strip about 125–175 g/4–6 oz/3/4–1 cup meat from the knuckle and chop it finely.

5 Add the chopped ham and vinegar to the soup and season to taste.

6 Bring back to the boil and simmer for 3–4 minutes. Serve.

VARIATION

If preferred, this soup can be sieved (strained) or blended in a food processor or blender until smooth. You can add more or less any type of vegetable depending on what is available. Leeks, celeriac (celery root), or chopped or canned tomatoes are particularly good.

MULLIGATAWNY SOUP

This warming soup, which is based on Madras curry, became popular with army officers in India at the beginning of the century, when they carried flasks of it into the cold hills for sustenance.

STEP 1

STEP 3

STEP 4

STEP 5

SERVES 4–6

45 g/1½ oz/3 tbsp butter or margarine
1 large onion, chopped
2 carrots, chopped
2–3 celery sticks, chopped
1 dessert apple, peeled, cored and chopped
1 tbsp plain (all-purpose) flour
1–2 tsp Madras curry powder
1–2 tsp curry paste
½ tsp ground coriander
1.25 litres/2¼ pints/5 cups Beef, Chicken or Vegetable Stock (see pages 76–8)
225 g/7 oz can chopped tomatoes
60 g/2 oz/½ cup cooked long grain rice (optional)
60–90 g/2–3 oz/⅓–½ cup cooked chicken, beef or lamb, chopped very finely
salt and pepper
poppadoms to serve (optional)

1 Melt the butter or margarine in a large saucepan and fry the onion, carrots, celery and apple, stirring occasionally, until just soft and lightly browned.

2 Stir in the flour, curry powder, curry paste and coriander and cook for a minute or so, stirring all the time.

3 Gradually add the stock and bring to the boil, stirring constantly. Add the tomatoes and plenty of seasoning, cover the pan and simmer for about 45 minutes until the vegetables and apple are very tender.

4 Cool the soup a little, then press through a sieve (strainer) or blend in a food processor or blender until smooth. Pour into a clean pan.

5 Add the rice, if using, and the chicken or meat, adjust the seasoning and bring to the boil. Simmer gently for 5 minutes.

6 Serve the soup in warmed bowls, with poppadoms, if liked.

FREEZING

This soup may be frozen for a maximum of 1 month; the spices may cause it to taste musty if stored for any longer.

MAKING SOUPS

The obvious accompaniment to a soup or broth is fresh crusty bread such as French, Italian, rye, oatmeal or mixed grain. Breads flavoured with olives, onions, walnuts, mixed seeds and cheese, and rolls of all shapes and sizes can also be served. The important thing is that the bread is very fresh, and it is often best served warm.

GARLIC BREAD
Cut a long French loaf in half, or use two short French loaves or a Vienna (rather fatter loaf). Blend about 125 g/4 oz/½ cup butter with 3–6 crushed garlic cloves. Cut the loaf into slanting slices about 2.5 cm/ 1 inch thick, leaving a hinge on the base crust. Spread each slice with the butter, reshape the loaf and wrap securely in foil. Before serving, place in a preheated oven at 200–220°C/400–425°F/Gas Mark 6–7 for about 20 minutes until hot and crisp. Fold back the foil and allow each guest to pull off slices as required.

Variations
Herb bread: Mix 3 tablespoons chopped fresh herbs (one type or mixed) or 1½ tablespoons dried herbs with the butter.

Anchovy bread: Mix a well drained and finely chopped can of anchovy fillets, a small jar of Gentleman's Relish or 70 g/ 2½ oz anchovy paste with the butter.

Making soup is one of the most satisfying cookery techniques: it is simple to do yet always produces tasty results. A wide range of ingredients can be used and it is easy to make substitutions when certain ingredients are not available. Soup making is also an excellent way of using up leftovers, whether the bones or carcass of roast meat or poultry, or cooked meat or vegetables.

STOCKS
The secret of a good soup lies in preparing a very good stock to use for the base, and although there are excellent stock cubes of all flavours readily available, it is home-made stock that puts the edge on any soup.

Stocks can be made in a variety of flavours and colours. A light or white stock requires raw, light-coloured bones, preferably veal, but these are not always available, so lamb and beef bones may also be used. For a darker stock it is necessary to use beef bones that have been roasted, so they darken. A poultry stock using chicken or turkey bones and carcasses is also light coloured, but if you use game carcasses, the stock will be darker and much stronger in flavour. To make fish stock, use fish heads, tails and trimmings, including the skin. You can buy fish trimmings from a fishmonger.

Bones alone are not sufficient for a good stock; you will also need a couple of chopped or sliced onions and two or three root vegetables, such as carrots, swede (rutabaga) or turnips, but avoid potatoes as they break up and make the stock cloudy. Celery and leeks can also be included. Flavourings such as one or two bay leaves may be added (use fresh ones if they are available as they have a better flavour) or a Bouquet Garni (see page 78), but do not add any seasoning (it should be added when the soup is made and depends on the other ingredients).

Put all the ingredients in a large saucepan, with the measured amount of water or enough to cover the contents of the pan: usually 1.75– 2.25 litres/3– 4 pints/1½ quarts–2 quarts. Once the water comes to the boil it is essential to remove the scum that forms on the surface, using a perforated spoon, before covering the pan and simmering for the recommended time. Fish stock should be simmered for only 30 minutes, as overcooking will give it a slightly bitter taste. Vegetable stock needs one hour's cooking, but all other stocks need at least 2 hours, and for beef bones 3–4 hours is best. A pressure cooker is an ideal appliance for making stock: simply follow the manufacturer's instructions.

General-purpose stock
about 1 kg/2 lb bones from a cooked joint or raw chopped beef, lamb or veal bones
2 onions, studded with 6 cloves, or sliced or chopped coarsely
2 carrots, sliced
1 leek, sliced
1–2 celery sticks, sliced
1 Bouquet Garni (see page 78)
about 2.25 litres/4 pints/2 quarts water

Chop or break up the bones and place in a large saucepan with the other ingredients. Bring to the boil and remove any scum from the surface with a perforated spoon. Cover and simmer gently for 3–4 hours. Strain the stock and leave to cool. Remove any fat from the surface and chill. If stored for more than 24 hours the stock must be boiled every day, cooled quickly and chilled again. The stock may be frozen for up to 2 months; place in a large plastic bag and seal, leaving at least 2.5 cm/1 inch of headspace to allow for expansion.

White stock
Make as above but use knuckle of veal, veal bones or raw lamb or beef bones and add a sliced lemon to the stockpot.

Brown beef stock
Use chopped marrow bones with a few strips of shin of beef if possible. Put in a roasting tin and cook in a preheated oven at 230°C/450°F/Gas Mark 8 for 30–50 minutes until browned. Transfer to a large saucepan, add the vegetables and water and continue as before.

Chicken, turkey or game stock
1 raw or cooked carcass of a chicken, turkey or 1–2 game birds
giblets, if available
2 onions, sliced or chopped
2 carrots, sliced
2–4 celery sticks, sliced
1 Bouquet Garni (see page 78) or 2–3 fresh or dried bay leaves

Break up the carcasses and place in a large saucepan with the remaining ingredients. Add enough water to cover. Bring to the boil, remove any scum and simmer for 2–3 hours. It is a good idea to give the bones a good stir and break them up a little during cooking. Strain, cool and store as for general-purpose stock.

Fish stock
1 head of a cod or salmon, etc, plus the trimmings, skin and bones or just the trimmings, skin and bones
1–2 onions, sliced
1 carrot, sliced
1–2 celery sticks, sliced
good squeeze of lemon juice
1 Bouquet Garni (see page 78) or 2 fresh or dried bay leaves

Wash the fish head and trimmings and place in a saucepan. Cover with water and bring to the boil. Remove any scum with a perforated spoon, then add the remaining ingredients. Cover and simmer for about 30 minutes. Strain and cool. Store in the refrigerator and use within 2 days.

Vegetable stock
To make vegetable stock you need a good selection of green and root vegetables, including onion and, if possible, leeks, but not potatoes. Take care when using very strongly flavoured vegetables such as celeriac (celery root) and artichokes as they will overpower the others. Coarsely chop about 500 g/1 lb mixed vegetables,

Curry bread: Mix 2–3 teaspoons curry powder with the butter.

POPPADOMS
These are ideal fried or grilled (broiled) and served with curry-flavoured soups such as Mulligatawny Soup (see page 74) or, indeed, any soup. Use either plain or flavoured poppadoms, and cut or break into smaller pieces before frying. They can be prepared earlier in the day.

SCONES
Warm scones with savoury flavours and toppings make excellent accompaniments to soups, especially when freshly made and served warm.

250 g/8 oz/2 cups self-raising flour
60 g/2 oz/¼ cup butter or margarine
1 egg, beaten
good squeeze lemon juice
about 75 ml/3 fl oz/⅓ cup milk
salt and pepper

Sift together the flour and seasoning, then rub in the butter or margarine until the mixture resembles fine breadcrumbs. Add the egg and lemon juice and enough milk to bind to a soft dough. Turn onto a floured surface and flatten out with your hands to about 2 cm/¾ inch thick. Either shape into a bar or cut into rounds, squares, triangles or fingers and place on a floured baking sheet. Dredge with flour or glaze with beaten egg or milk. Sprinkle with sesame, pumpkin, sunflower or poppy seeds, finely chopped or flaked nuts, grated cheese, crumbled crisp bacon, or oatmeal, if liked. Bake in a preheated oven at 220°C/425°F/Gas Mark 7 for about 15 minutes for individual scones or 20–25 minutes for a scone bar. Cool slightly on a wire rack before serving.

Variations
Herb scones: Add 2 tbsp chopped fresh herbs (one type or mixed) or 2 teaspoons dried herbs.

Cheese scones: Add 90 g/3 oz/ ⅓ cup grated blue or mature (sharp) Cheddar cheese or 3 tablespoons grated Parmesan cheese.

Anchovy scones: Add a drained and minced can of anchovy fillets

Nut scones: Add 60 g/2 oz/ scant ½ cup finely chopped walnuts, pecan nuts, hazelnuts or almonds.

Bacon scones: Add 90 g/3 oz/ scant ½ cup minced (ground) lean bacon.

cover generously with water, cover and simmer for about 1 hour. Strain and keep in the refrigerator for up to 24 hours.

BOUQUET GARNI
A bouquet garni is simply a bunch of herbs which is used to give flavour to stocks, soups, stews and sauces. The herbs can be made into a small bunch and tied with string, or they can be tied in muslin (cheesecloth), which is essential if you include dried herbs, cloves or peppercorns, as they should be easy to remove before serving. Herbs such as rosemary, sage, fennel and dill can be used but remember that these are very strongly flavoured and must blend with the dish to be made.

Traditional bouquet garni
1 fresh or dried bay leaf
few sprigs of fresh parsley
few sprigs of fresh thyme

Tie the herbs together with a length of string or cotton.

Dried bouquet garni
1 dried bay leaf
good pinch of dried mixed herbs or any one herb
good pinch of dried parsley
8–10 black peppercorns
2–4 cloves
1 garlic clove (optional)

Put all the ingredients in a small square of muslin (cheesecloth) and secure with string or cotton, leaving a long tail so it can be tied to the handle of the pan for easy removal.

GARNISHES
The appearance of a soup can be greatly enhanced by a suitable garnish. The simplest garnishes are chopped herbs, which can be added to the soup itself and sprinkled on top. The type of herb should complement the flavour of the soup, but parsley and chives blend with almost any type. Whole leaves and small sprigs of herbs such as mint, oregano, fennel and dill can also be used as they will float on the surface. Dried herbs are not an attractive garnish but can be added to the soup during cooking.

Lemon, orange or lime rind can be grated or cut into fine strips. Coarsely grated rind or strips should be blanched in boiling water for 2–3 minutes if they are to be eaten. With care, they too will float on the surface. Very thin slices of lemon or lime can also be floated on top of soups, particularly chilled ones.

Vegetables such as carrots, turnips, swede (rutabaga) and celeriac (celery root) can be coarsely grated into a soup just before serving, to add colour and texture. Leeks can be cut into very thin rings and used either raw or blanched. Fried thin onion rings and blanched or lightly fried, thinly sliced mushrooms can also be used as garnishes. Coarsely grated cheese such as Cheddar, Leicester (red), Gruyère (Swiss) and Stilton (blue) are good sprinkled over soups. Very crisply fried or grilled (broiled) bacon can be crumbled and used as a garnish.

Croûtons
These can be served separately, to be sprinkled on the soup by your guests or placed on each portion before serving.

Toasted croûtons
Toast slices of bread and cut into cubes, triangles or other shapes while hot. Cocktail cutters or aspic cutters will allow you to cut out a variety of shapes. Allow to cool. They can be stored in an airtight container for two to three days.

Fried croûtons
These are best cut into shapes before cooking. Fry in shallow oil for a few minutes, turning until golden on both sides. The oil must be hot, but take care as the bread will brown very quickly. Drain on paper towels. Croûtons may be dipped in chopped herbs, paprika or chopped hard-boiled (hard-cooked) egg.

Garlic croûtons
Make as for fried croûtons, adding 3–4 crushed garlic cloves to the oil.

Pastry crescents
Crescents or other shapes can be cut from puff or shortcrust pastry, glazed with beaten egg or milk and topped with sesame seeds, poppy seeds or finely chopped nuts. Bake in a preheated oven at 200°C/400°F/Gas Mark 6 for about 10 minutes until golden brown.

Garnishes for consommé
This clear soup is traditionally served with a garnish of freshly cooked tiny pasta shapes, noodles, rice, lightly cooked diced or julienne of vegetables, or thinly sliced mushrooms. Or make a one-egg omelette, drain thoroughly on paper towels, then cut into strips or shapes.

THICKENING SOUPS
A variety of thickening agents can be used, depending on the type of soup.

Cream
To prevent curdling, put the cream in a basin, add a little of the hot soup, then stir into the soup. Reheat gently but don't allow it to boil.

Flour and cornflour (cornstarch)
Blend plain (all-purpose) flour or cornflour (cornstarch) with a little cold milk or water, add a little of the hot soup, then whisk back into the soup. Simmer for a few minutes, until thickened.

Beurre manié
Blend equal quantities of sifted plain (all-purpose) flour and butter or margarine, then whisk small amounts into the soup, until blended. Simmer for 3–4 minutes.

Egg yolks
Blend egg yolks with a little milk or cream, then add a little of the soup. Strain the mixture into the soup, off the heat, whisking thoroughly. Reheat gently but do not allow to boil.

CHEESE & ANCHOVY TWISTS
Unroll a packet of thawed ready-rolled puff pastry and cut in half lengthwise. Spread one piece evenly with Gentleman's Relish or anchovy paste, then cover evenly with about 175 g/ 6 oz /1½ cups finely grated Gouda or Emmental (Swiss) cheese. A little grated Parmesan cheese may also be sprinkled over. Place the other piece of pastry on top and press together firmly. Using a sharp knife and ruler, cut into strips about 1 cm/½ inch wide. If liked, brush with beaten egg or milk. Give each strip two twists and place on a greased baking sheet. Shape the ends into points and make sure they are evenly shaped all over. Bake in a preheated oven at 200°C/400°F/Gas Mark 6 for about 15 minutes until well puffed up and golden brown. Serve warm or cold. The twists may be frozen for up to 1 month.

INDEX